MASTERING DIGITAL MARKETING
Advanced Strategies for the
Modern Marketer

Comfort Ojukwu

Mastering Digital Marketing
Advanced Strategies for the Modern Marketer

Cover Design:
Comfort Ojukwu

Publisher: BoD · Books on Demand GmbH, Überseering 33,
22297 Hamburg, bod@bod.de
Print: Libri Plureos GmbH, Friedensallee 273, 22763 Hamburg
ISBN: 978-3-8192-7661-3

This publication may contain references to tools and platforms that incorporate artificial intelligence (AI). AI-powered tools were also utilized
during the research and creation of this book to streamline data analysis,
optimize content structuring, and enhance accuracy.

AI Contributions:
This book was supported by AI technologies for data-driven research,
content organization, and proofreading, ensuring clarity, precision, and
the integration of cutting-edge marketing insights. Tools used include:

-AI-powered content generation for initial drafts.
-Grammar and style checks with AI editing tools.
-Data visualization tools for analytics and trends.

FOREWARD

The digital marketing world evolves rapidly, presenting both exciting opportunities and complex challenges. Mastering Digital Marketing: Advanced Strategies for the Modern Marketer is your guide to thriving in this landscape.

Blending foundational principles with advanced techniques, this book covers everything from AI and blockchain to SEO and social media, ensuring you stay ahead. It also emphasizes ethical practices and practical frameworks for innovative, responsible marketing.

Whether refining your expertise or starting fresh, this book equips you to excel and lead in the digital age.

Here's to your success in mastering modern marketing.

CONTENTS

SPECIALIZED AREAS AND ETHICAL CONSIDERATIONS

APPENDIX B 108

Glossary of Digital Marketing Terms

APPENDIX C 110

Templates and Frameworks

Part I: Foundations of Digital Marketing

CHAPTER ONE
THE EVOLUTION OF DIGITAL MARKETING

From Traditional to Digital: A Historical Overview

The journey of marketing has undergone a transformative evolution over the decades. Traditional marketing, rooted in print, radio, television, and direct mail, was primarily a one-way communication channel. Brands spoke, and consumers listened. This paradigm, while effective in its time, lacked the personalization, interactivity, and measurability that define digital marketing today.

The late 20th century marked the initial transition from traditional to digital marketing. With the advent of personal computers in the 1980s and the proliferation of the internet in the 1990s, businesses gained new avenues to reach consumers. Email marketing emerged as one of the first digital marketing tools, paving the way for direct, measurable communication. Search engines like Yahoo and Google (launched in 1994 and 1998, respectively) redefined how information was accessed and introduced the importance of visibility on the web.

The 2000s saw the rise of social media platforms such as Facebook (2004), YouTube (2005), and

Twitter (2006), transforming the internet from a static information repository to an interactive, community-driven space. The smartphone revolution, catalyzed by the iPhone in 2007, further shifted the landscape, making marketing truly omnipresent. Today, digital marketing is an ecosystem where brands not only promote products but also foster relationships, build trust, and create personalized experiences.

Key Milestones in Digital Marketing Development
   Digital marketing's evolution is marked by key technological and cultural milestones:
   1. 1990s: The Foundations
       *   Launch of the World Wide Web and early websites.
       *   Introduction of email marketing and banner ads (e.g., AT&T's banner ad on HotWired in 1994).
       *   Emergence of SEO practices with the first search engines.
   2. 2000s: The Social and Mobile Era
       *   Rise of blogging as a marketing tool (e.g., Blogger in 1999).
       *   Search engine advertising took off with Google Ads in 2000.
       *   Launch of major social media platforms like LinkedIn (2003) and Facebook (2004).
       *   The first mobile marketing campaigns, driven by SMS and later app-based advertising.
   3. 2010s: Personalization and Automation
       *   Content marketing matured, with storytelling and thought leadership becoming central to brand strategy.
       *   Programmatic advertising and marketing

automation tools streamlined campaign management.
- Video marketing boomed with platforms like YouTube and later TikTok (2016).
4. 2020s: The AI Revolution
   - AI-driven tools for personalization and predictive analytics.
   - Voice search optimization in response to smart assistants like Alexa and Google Home.
   - The emergence of the metaverse, NFTs, and blockchain technologies, pushing boundaries of digital engagement.

The Role of AI and Emerging Technologies

Artificial intell gence (AI) is arguably the most transformative force in digital marketing today. By analyzing vast amounts of data, AI enables businesses to understand consumer behavior at an unprecedented scale. Here are some ways AI and emerging technologies are reshaping the digital marketing landscape:

1. Personalization
   AI-driven algorithms power hyper-personalized recommer dations, ensuring that consumers receive content, products, or services tailored to their preferences and behavior. Platforms like Netflix anc Amazon are leaders in this space.
2. Automation
   Marketing automation tools, powered by AI, streamline repetitive tasks like email campaigns, social media scheduling, and ad placements, allowing marketers to focus on strategy and creativity.

3. Voice and Visual Search
   The rise of voice search, fueled by smart assistants like Siri and Alexa, has compelled marketers to optimize for natural language queries. Similarly, visual search tools like Google Lens are changing how consumers discover products.
4. The Metaverse and Virtual Reality
   Platforms like Roblox and Meta (formerly Facebook) are creating virtual spaces where brands can engage consumers through immersive experiences. Virtual showrooms, events, and gamified campaigns are just the beginning.
5. Blockchain and Transparency
   Blockchain technology ensures transparency and trust in digital advertising by reducing fraud and providing verifiable data. It is also the backbone of NFTs, which brands are using to create unique digital assets and experiences.
6. Predictive Analytics and Insights
   By leveraging machine learning, businesses can predict future trends, anticipate customer needs, and make data-driven decisions with greater accuracy.

As digital marketing continues to evolve, embracing these technologies will be essential for businesses to stay competitive and connect with their audiences effectively.

CHAPTER TWO
UNDERSTANDING DIGITAL CONSUMER BEHAVIOR

The Psychology of Online Engagement

Online engagement is deeply rooted in psychological principles that drive human behavior. Digital consumers are not merely rational decision-makers; they are emotional beings influenced by a mix of cognitive biases, social proof, and intrinsic motivators. Marketers who understand these psychological triggers can design campaigns that resonate deeply with their audience.

1. Emotional Triggers:
   Content that evokes strong emotions—whether joy, surprise, or even fear—tends to perform better. Emotional storytelling, coupled with relatable visuals and narratives, creates lasting impressions and drives shares.
2. Cognitive Biases:
   - FOMO (Fear of Missing Out): Limited-time offers or exclusive deals tap into consumers' fear of missing an opportunity.
   - Anchoring Effect: Highlighting an original price alongside a discounted price can anchor the perceived value of a product.

- Reciprocity: Offering free value, such as eBooks or trial periods, encourages consumers to give back by purchasing or engaging.
3. Social Proof:
   Online reviews, user-generated content, and influencer endorsements provide the validation many consumers seek before making a decision.
4. The Role of Personalization:
   Personalization makes users feel understood, increasing their emotional connection with a brand. AI-driven personalization, such as product recommendations or tailored email content, ensures relevance and boosts engagement.

Digital Customer Journeys and Decision-Making Processes

The digital customer journey has become increasingly non-linear, with consumers interacting with multiple touchpoints across various devices and platforms before making a purchase decision. Understanding this journey is key to designing seamless and engaging experiences.

1. Stages of the Digital Customer Journey:
   - Awareness: The consumer identifies a need or becomes aware of a product or service through ads, social media, or search engines.
   - Consideration: Research begins as consumers compare options, read reviews, and seek recommendations.
   - Decision: A purchase is made, often influenced by price, convenience, or trust in the brand.
   - Post-Purchase: The journey continues with feedback, reviews, and the potential for repeat purchases or advocacy.
3. Micro-Moments in Decision-Making:

Google's concept of "micro-moments" highlights the importance of being present during key instances when consumers seek information, decide what to buy, or finalize a purchase. These include:

- I-want-to-know moments: Research-oriented actions.
- I-want-to-go moments: Location-based searches.
- I-want-to-do moments: Tutorials or instructional content.
- I-want-to-buy moments: Purchase intent actions.

5. Omnichannel Experiences:
   Consumers expect a cohesive experience across all touchpoints—whether it's a website, app, email, or physical store. An integrated approach ensures brand consistency and enhances trust.
7. The Role of Trust and Transparency:
   - Transparent practices, such as clear pricing and data usage policies, foster trust.
   - Offering customer reviews and testimonials helps reduce perceived risk during the decision-making process.

Behavioral Data Analytics

Behavioral data analytics involves analyzing how consumers interact with digital platforms to uncover patterns, preferences, and opportunities for optimization. It empowers marketers to make data-driven decisions and create more effective campaigns.

1. Types of Behavioral Data:
   - Clickstream Data: Tracks every click and interaction on a website or app.
   - Engagement Metrics: Includes likes, shares,

comments, and time spent on content.
- Transactional Data: Analyzes purchase history, cart abandonment rates, and subscription trends.
- Survey and Feedback Data: Captures direct input from consumers.

2. Tools for Behavioral Analysis:
   - Google Analytics: Provides detailed insights into website traffic and user behavior.
   - Hotjar: Offers heatmaps and session recordings to visualize how users navigate a site.
   - Mixpanel: Tracks user interactions within apps or websites for in-depth behavioral analysis.

3. Applications of Behavioral Analytics:
   - Segmentation: Grouping users based on behavior (e.g., frequent buyers, one-time visitors) for targeted campaigns.
   - Personalization: Delivering tailored experiences based on past actions and preferences.
   - Predictive Modeling: Using historical data to anticipate future behaviors, such as churn likelihood or purchase intent.

4. Ethical Considerations:
   While behavioral analytics offers incredible potential, ethical practices are essential. Transparency about data collection, adhering to privacy laws like GDPR, and respecting consumer preferences are crucial for building trust and maintaining compliance.

Understanding digital consumer behavior is a blend of psychology, strategic mapping of the customer journey, and leveraging behavioral data analytics. By mastering these elements, marketers can create highly relevant and impactful experiences that guide consumers from awareness to advocacy seamlessly.

CHAPTER THREE
THE CORE PILLARS OF DIGITAL MARKETING

Content Marketing
Content is the foundation of digital marketing, serving as the medium through which brands engage, educate, and persuade their audience. Effective content marketing is centered on creating and distributing valuable, relevant, and consistent content to attract and retain a defined audience.

1. Key Elements of Content Marketing:
   - Blog Posts: Informative articles that address customer pain points and establish authority.
   - E-books and Whitepapers: In-depth resources for lead generation and thought leadership.
   - Video Content: Highly engaging content that drives traffic and conversion rates.
   - Infographics: Visual representations of complex data or concepts.
2. Benefits of Content Marketing:
   - Builds trust and brand loyalty.
   - Enhances SEO performance by driving organic traffic.
   - Provides value at every stage of the customer

journey.
3. Key Tools:
    - HubSpot for content strategy and management.
    - Canva for creating visual content.
    - SEMrush for identifying content opportunities.

Social Media Marketing

Social media platforms are crucial for building brand awareness, engaging with audiences, and driving traffic. Each platform serves a different purpose and audience segment, requiring tailored strategies.

1. Key Platforms and Their Strengths:
    - Facebook: Broad reach, ideal for community building and targeted advertising.
    - Instagram: Visual storytelling through photos, videos, and reels.
    - LinkedIn: Best for B2B marketing and professional networking.
    - TikTok: Short-form video content for younger, trend-driven audiences.
2. Strategies for Success:
    - Consistent posting and engagement with followers.
    - Using analytics to refine content based on performance.
    - Leveraging paid promotions for extended reach.
3. Key Tools:
    - Buffer or Hootsuite for scheduling posts.
    - Sprout Social for analytics and reporting.
    - Later for visual-first platforms like Instagram and Pinterest.

Search Engine Optimization (SEO)

SEO ensures that your content ranks high in search engine results, driving organic traffic and increasing visibility. It involves both on-page and off-page optimization.

1. Key Components of SEO:
   - Keyword Research: Identifying and targeting terms your audience searches for.
   - On-Page SEO: Optimizing meta tags, headers, and content for target keywords.
   - Off-Page SEO: Building high-quality backlinks and maintaining a strong online reputation.
   - Technical SEO: Ensuring fast page loading speeds, mobile-friendliness, and clean site architecture.
2. Emerging Trends in SEO:
   - Voice search optimization with conversational keywords.
   - Focus on E-A-T (Expertise, Authority, Trustworthiness) for content quality.
   - AI-powered search algorithms like Google's RankBrain.
3. Key Tools:
   - Ahrefs or SEMrush for keyword and competitor analysis.
   - Yoast SEO for WordPress optimization.
   - Google Search Console for technical insights.

Pay-Per-Click Advertising (PPC)

PPC advertising is a model where advertisers pay each time their ad is clicked. It is an effective way to drive immediate traffic and leads, especially for competitive keywords.

1. Key Platforms:

- Google Ads: Dominates the search engine advertising space.
- Facebook Ads: Enables detailed audience targeting for visual and text-based ads.
- LinkedIn Ads: Best for targeting B2B professionals.

2. Advantages of PPC:
   - Immediate visibility for new products or services.
   - Precise targeting based on demographics, location, and behavior.
   - Measurable ROI through analytics and conversion tracking.

3. Key Tools:
   - Google Keyword Planner for ad strategy.
   - Adzooma for campaign management across platforms.
   - Optmyzr for automation and optimization of PPC campaigns.

Email Marketing

Email remains one of the highest ROI-generating digital marketing channels. It allows businesses to maintain direct communication with their audience.

1. Types of Email Campaigns:
   - Welcome Emails: First impressions for new subscribers.
   - Newsletters: Regular updates and curated content.
   - Drip Campaigns: Automated series to nurture leads.
   - Promotional Emails: Deals, discounts, and limited-time offers.

2. Best Practices:
   - Personalize subject lines and content.
   - Optimize for mobile devices.
   - Use A/B testing to refine email performance.
3. Key Tools:
   - Mailchimp for automation and analytics.
   - Constant Contact for campaign management.
   - ConvertKit for creators and influencers.

Affiliate and Influencer Marketing

Affiliate and influencer marketing leverage partnerships to promote products or services, expanding reach and driving conversions.

1. Affiliate Marketing:
   - Involves collaborating with affiliates who promote your products in exchange for a commission on sales.
   - Commonly used in industries like e-commerce and SaaS.
2. Influencer Marketing:
   - Partners with individuals who have large, engaged audiences on social media.
   - Effective for reaching niche markets and building brand credibility.
3. Strategies for Success:
   - Vet affiliates and influencers for brand alignment.
   - Provide creatives and clear guidelines for promotion.
   - Track performance through unique links or promo codes.
4. Key Tools:
   - ShareASale or CJ Affiliate for affiliate program

management.
- Upfluence or AspireIQ for identifying and managing influencers.
- BuzzSumo for finding trending influencers in your niche.

These core pillars of digital marketing form a cohesive framework for reaching and engaging audiences. While each pillar serves a distinct purpose, their combined impact ensures a robust and well-rounded digital marketing strategy. By mastering these elements, marketers can maximize ROI and foster long-term brand success.

Part II: Advanced Content and SEO Strategies

CHAPTER FOUR
CONTENT MARKETING IN DEPTH

Advanced Content Creation Techniques

Creating standout content requires more than basic writing skills—it demands innovation, relevance, and a deep understanding of the audience. Advanced techniques help marketers produce content that not only captures attention but also drives action.

1. Data-Driven Content:
   - Leverage analytics tools like Google Analytics or BuzzSumo to identify trending topics and gaps in existing content.
   - Use proprietary data or surveys to create unique, authoritative insights.
2. Cluster Content Model:
   - Organize content into pillar pages (comprehensive guides) supported by topic clusters (related subtopics).
   - Improves SEO by creating interlinked, authoritative content ecosystems.
3. Multiformat Content:
   - Repurpose long-form content into various formats such as infographics, podcasts, videos,

and social media posts to reach different audience segments.
- Tools like Canva and Pictory can streamline this process.

4. AI-Enhanced Content Creation:
   - Use AI tools like Jasper, Grammarly, or ChatGPT to generate, refine, and optimize content efficiently.
   - Ensure AI-generated content is personalized and aligns with brand voice.

Storytelling for Brands

Storytelling is a powerful tool that allows brands to connect emotionally with their audience, build trust, and inspire action.

1. Core Elements of Effective Brand Stories:
   - Relatable Characters: Craft personas that resonate with your target audience.
   - Conflict and Resolution: Present challenges that your brand or product helps to solve.
   - Emotional Appeal: Use stories to evoke empathy, excitement, or inspiration.

2. Formats for Brand Storytelling:
   - Case Studies: Showcase real-world examples of how your product or service solved a problem.
   - Behind-the-Scenes Content: Offer a glimpse into your company culture or production process.
   - Customer Stories: Highlight testimonials or user-generated content that humanizes your brand.

3. Digital Storytelling Techniques:
   - Use interactive tools like Instagram Stories,

TikTok, or immersive video formats to create dynamic narratives.
- Leverage long-form blogs or email series to tell sequential stories that keep audiences engaged.

Interactive and Immersive Content

Interactive and immersive content transforms passive viewers into active participants, enhancing engagement and retention.

1. Types of Interactive Content:
   - Quizzes and Polls: Engage users while gathering valuable data about preferences and behaviors.
   - Calculators: Provide personalized results, such as ROI calculators for B2B or budget planners for consumers.
   - Interactive Infographics: Allow users to explore data through clickable, dynamic elements.
2. Emerging Trends in Immersive Content:
   - Augmented Reality (AR): Virtual try-ons for fashion or furniture brands using tools like Snapchat AR or Shopify AR.
   - Virtual Reality (VR): Create fully immersive brand experiences, such as virtual showrooms or tours.
   - 360-Degree Videos: Offer a panoramic view of products, events, or destinations.
3. Benefits of Interactive and Immersive Content:
   - Boosts engagement and dwell time on digital platforms.
   - Improves conversion rates by delivering personalized, memorable experiences.
   - Encourages social sharing due to its novelty and entertainment value.

4. Tools to Create Interactive Content:
    - Outgrow: Build interactive calculators and quizzes.
    - ThingLink: Create interactive images and videos.
    - Ceros: Design visually rich, interactive web experiences.

Mastering advanced content creation techniques, storytelling, and immersive formats ensures your content strategy remains competitive and impactful. By integrating these approaches, marketers can craft compelling narratives, foster deeper connections, and deliver meaningful experiences that captivate audiences and drive results.

CHAPTER FIVE
SEARCH ENGINE OPTIMIZATION (SEO)

Technical SEO and Site Performance Optimization

Technical SEO ensures that your website is optimized for search engine crawling, indexing, and ranking. It forms the backbone of a successful SEO strategy, improving user experience and search visibility.

1. Core Elements of Technical SEO:
   - Website Speed:
     - Optimize image sizes, use content delivery networks (CDNs), and implement lazy loading.
     - Tools like Google PageSpeed Insights or GTmetrix can identify performance bottlenecks.
   - Mobile-Friendliness:
     - Responsive design ensures seamless experiences across devices.
     - Test mobile usability with Google's Mobile-Friendly Test tool.
   - Crawlability and Indexability:
     - Ensure your site structure is clear and use XML sitemaps to help search engines navigate

your pages.
- Identify and fix issues like broken links or duplicate content with tools like Screaming Frog or Ahrefs.
- HTTPS and Security:
- Secure your site with SSL certificates to build trust and improve rankings.
- Structured Data (Schema Markup):
- Add schema markup to highlight key information, such as reviews, FAQs, and events, making it easier for search engines to understand your content.
2. Site Performance Optimization:
- Core Web Vitals: Focus on metrics like Largest Contentful Paint (LCP), First Input Delay (FID), and Cumulative Layout Shift (CLS) to enhance user experience.
- Server Optimization: Use faster hosting solutions and leverage server-side caching.
- Minimizing Scripts and Styles: Compress CSS, JavaScript, and HTML files.

Semantic Search and NLP Applications
Search engines increasingly rely on semantic search and natural language processing (NLP) to understand user intent and context, making SEO strategies more sophisticated.
3. Understanding Semantic Search:
- Focuses on understanding the meaning behind queries rather than matching exact keywords.
- Helps search engines deliver more accurate and contextually relevant results.
4. Optimizing for Semantic Search:

- Long-Tail Keywords: Use conversational phrases and natural language queries.
- Contextual Content: Create in-depth, topic-focused content that answers user queries comprehensively.
- Internal Linking: Strengthen content connections by linking related pages, aiding semantic understanding.
5. Natural Language Processing (NLP) in SEO:
   - Tools like Google's BERT (Bidirectional Encoder Representations from Transformers) analyze context in search queries.
   - Strategies to optimize for NLP:
   - Write content naturally and answer "how," "why," and "what" questions clearly.
   - Leverage FAQs to address specific user intents.
6. The Role of AI in Semantic SEO:
   - Use AI tools like MarketMuse or Clearscope to identify topic clusters and keyword variations that align with semantic trends.
   - Optimize content for featured snippets and voice search, focusing on concise and actionable answers.

Local SEO and International SEO

Local and international SEO strategies cater to specific geographic audiences, optimizing visibility for businesses targeting local markets or global audiences.
1. Local SEO Strategies:
   - Google Business Profile (GBP):
     - Claim and optimize your Google Business Profile with accurate business details, photos, and reviews.

- Use location-based keywords in descriptions and posts.
- Local Citations:
    - Ensure consistency across all online directories, such as Yelp, Bing Places, and Yellow Pages.
- Customer Reviews:
    - Encourage positive reviews on GBP and other platforms, as they impact rankings and credibility.
- Localized Content:
    - Create content tailored to local interests and events, incorporating geo-specific keywords.

2. International SEO Strategies:
- Hreflang Tags:
    - Implement hreflang tags to indicate language and regional targeting for global audiences.
- Multilingual Content:
    - Provide content in multiple languages using professional translation and localization services.
    - Tools like Weglot or WPML can simplify multilingual website management.
- Regional Domain Extensions:
    - Use country-specific top-level domains (TLDs), such as .de for Germany or .fr for France, to boost local relevance.
- Cultural Sensitivity:
    - Adapt images, colors, and messaging to align with local cultural norms.
- Global Keyword Research:
    - Use tools like SEMrush or Ahrefs to identify

region-specific keyword opportunities.
3. Challenges in Local and International SEO:
   - Balancing global brand consistency with local relevance.
   - Managing duplicate content across multiple regions.
   - Navigating legal and regulatory differences in various markets.

SEO is no longer just about ranking for keywords—it's about delivering a seamless, personalized, and technically sound experience for users across the globe. By mastering technical SEO, leveraging semantic search, and adapting strategies for local and international markets, businesses can position themselves for long-term search success.

CHAPTER SIX
VOICE AND VISUAL SEARCH OPTIMIZATION

The Rise of Smart Assistants

Smart assistants like Amazon Alexa, Google Assistant, Siri, and Cortana are reshaping how users interact with search engines. Voice search, driven by natural language queries, is transforming SEO strategies by prioritizing conversational and intent-driven content.

1. Key Drivers of Voice Search Growth:
    *   Device Proliferation: Smart speakers, smartphones, and IoT devices have made voice search more accessible.
    *   User Convenience: Hands-free, fast, and natural, voice search is popular for on-the-go queries.
    *   Advancements in AI and NLP: Technologies like Google's BERT and GPT have improved understanding of user intent.
2. Characteristics of Voice Search Queries:
    *   Conversational Language: Longer, natural-sounding phrases such as "What's the best Italian restaurant near me?"
    *   Question-Based Queries: Users frequently start

with "how," "what," "why," "where," or "when."

- Local Intent: Many voice searches involve local queries, such as finding businesses or directions.

3. Strategies for Voice Search Optimization:
   - Focus on Long-Tail Keywords: Incorporate phrases that mimic spoken language.
   - Create FAQ Content: Address common questions clearly and concisely in your content.
   - Optimize for Local SEO: Ensure your business details are accurate on Google Business Profile and other directories.
   - Leverage Structured Data: Use schema markup to make content easily digestible for smart assistants.
   - Improve Site Speed: Voice search users expect quick answers, so optimize loading times.

Strategies for Visual Content Optimization

Visual search is gaining traction as platforms like Google Lens, Pinterest, and Amazon empower users to search using images rather than text. Optimizing for visual search is critical to staying ahead in a visually driven digital landscape.

1. Key Drivers of Visual Search Growth:
   - Advancing AI and Image Recognition: Technologies like computer vision have improved object recognition accuracy.
   - Consumer Behavior: Shoppers increasingly use visual search to find products they see in real life or online.
   - Platform Support: Tools like Pinterest Lens and Google Images encourage visual search

adoption.
2. Optimizing Visual Content for Search:
  - High-Quality Images:
    - Use high-resolution, clear, and appealing images to increase engagement and ranking.
  - Descriptive File Names:
    - Rename image files with descriptive, keyword-rich names (e.g., "red-leather-sofa.jpg" instead of "IMG12345.jpg").
  - Alt Text:
    - Write concise, keyword-focused alt text to describe images for search engines and improve accessibility.
  - Image Compression:
    - Use tools like TinyPNG or ImageOptim to reduce file sizes without sacrificing quality, ensuring faster load times.
  - Add Structured Data:
    - Implement schema markup for images, particularly for product and recipe content, to enhance search visibility.
3. Emerging Visual Search Trends:
  - Augmented Reality (AR): Platforms like Instagram and Snapchat enable users to try on products virtually, creating immersive shopping experiences.
  - Product Tags in Visual Content: Tag products in images to direct users to purchasing options, especially on platforms like Pinterest and Instagram.
  - 3D and 360-Degree Images: Interactive visuals give users a detailed view of products, boosting

engagement and conversion rates.
4. Tools for Visual Content Optimization:
   - Google Lens: Analyze how users discover your brand through image searches.
   - Canva and Adobe Photoshop: Enhance visual appeal and customize images for different platforms.
   - Pinterest Analytics: Monitor performance of pins and trends in visual content.

Voice and visual search are no longer emerging trends—they are integral parts of how users engage with digital platforms. By optimizing for conversational voice queries and crafting visually rich, search-friendly content, brands can tap into these dynamic search channels, driving traffic, engagement, and conversions. These strategies ensure you stay ahead in an evolving SEO landscape.

PART III: PAID MEDIA AND ANALYTICS

CHAPTER SEVEN
PAY-PER-CLICK (PPC) CAMPAIGNS

Advanced Google Ads Strategies

Google Ads remains a cornerstone of PPC advertising, offering unparalleled reach and targeting capabilities. Advanced strategies help marketers maximize ROI by refining audience targeting, ad relevance, and bidding efficiency.

1. Dynamic Search Ads (DSAs):
   - Automatically generate ads based on your website's content to fill keyword gaps.
   - Ideal for large e-commerce sites or businesses with rapidly changing inventories.
2. Ad Customizers:
   - Use dynamic parameters like location, time, or user behavior to create highly personalized ad experiences.
   - For example, "50% off laptops in [City] today only!"
3. Enhanced Audience Targeting:
   - Combine in-market audiences with custom intent audiences to target users actively

researching your product or service.
- Layer demographic and behavioral targeting for precise reach.
4. Smart Bidding Strategies:
    - Utilize machine learning for automated bidding strategies like Target ROAS (Return on Ad Spend) or Maximize Conversions.
    - Continuously test and refine bidding settings based on campaign goals.
5. A/B Testing and Experimentation:
    - Test multiple versions of ad copy, visuals, and landing pages to identify top performers.
    - Use Google Ads' Drafts and Experiments feature for controlled testing environments.
6. YouTube Ads Integration:
    - Leverage video ads to complement search campaigns, targeting users at various stages of the funnel.

Leveraging AI in PPC Campaigns

AI-driven tools and strategies are revolutionizing PPC management, offering smarter targeting, optimization, and campaign insights.
1. Automated Campaign Management:
    - Use platforms like Google's Performance Max campaigns that rely on AI to serve ads across multiple channels (search, display, YouTube, etc.).
    - Optimize creatives and targeting in real-time based on performance data.
2. Predictive Analytics:
    - Predict user behavior and campaign outcomes using tools like Adzooma or Marin Software.

- Identify high-value segments and optimize budget allocation accordingly.
3. AI-Enhanced Ad Copy and Creatives:
   - Tools like Jasper and Copy.ai can generate persuasive ad copy tailored to different audiences.
   - Canva AI or Google's Auto-Creatives feature helps produce visually appealing ad designs.
4. Keyword Discovery with AI:
   - Platforms like SEMrush and Ahrefs use AI to uncover long-tail keywords and competitive opportunities.
   - Automate negative keyword discovery to avoid wasted spend.
5. Budget Optimization:
   - AI tools such as Optmyzr help allocate budgets dynamically, prioritizing high-performing campaigns and pausing underperformers.

Retargeting and Lookalike Audiences

Retargeting and lookalike audiences enable advertisers to engage users who have shown interest or share similar traits with their existing customers. These strategies boost conversions by refining ad delivery to high-potential segments.
1. Retargeting Techniques:
   - Website Retargeting: Show ads to users who have visited your website but didn't convert.
   - Engagement Retargeting: Re-engage users who interacted with your ads, social media, or videos.
   - Dynamic Retargeting: Serve personalized ads featuring products users viewed on your site,

ideal for e-commerce.

2. Crafting Effective Retargeting Ads:
   - Highlight unique value propositions or limited-time offers to entice users back.
   - Use carousel ads to showcase multiple products relevant to user interests.
   - Incorporate social proof like customer reviews or testimonials.

3. Lookalike Audience Strategies:
   - Building Lookalikes: Use your customer database or website visitors as a seed audience to create lookalike segments.
   - Facebook and Instagram Ads: Leverage Meta's tools to find users who resemble your existing customers based on behavior and demographics.
   - Google Ads Similar Audiences: Target users with characteristics and online behaviors similar to your converters.

4. Combining Retargeting and Lookalike Audiences:
   - Use retargeting to nurture warm leads and lookalikes to expand your reach to similar potential customers.
   - Pair strategies with time-sensitive offers to drive urgency.

5. Tracking and Measurement:
   - Use tools like Google Analytics, Meta Pixel, and CRM platforms to measure audience engagement and conversion rates.
   - Continuously refine retargeting and lookalike campaigns based on performance metrics like CTR, CPA, and ROI.

Advanced PPC strategies, combined with AI innovations and audience-focused tactics like retargeting and lookalike audiences, empower advertisers to achieve superior campaign performance. By tailoring ads to specific user behaviors and leveraging cutting-edge tools, businesses can maximize their PPC investments and drive sustained growth.

CHAPTER EIGHT
SOCIAL MEDIA ADVERTISING

Platform-Specific Strategies

Social media advertising offers diverse opportunities across platforms, each with unique strengths, audience demographics, and advertising tools. Crafting tailored strategies for each platform is essential for maximizing impact.

1. Meta (Facebook and Instagram):
   - Ad Formats: Carousel ads, Stories, Reels, and collection ads for immersive experiences.
   - Audience Targeting: Leverage Meta's robust targeting options, including interest-based, behavioral, and lookalike audiences.
   - Creative Best Practices:
     - Use visually appealing content that fits seamlessly into users' feeds.
     - Incorporate short captions and call-to-actions (CTAs) like "Shop Now" or "Learn More."
   - Key Features:
     - Dynamic Ads: Showcase personalized products based on user browsing behavior.

- Retargeting: Re-engage users who have interacted with your website or previous ads.
2. TikTok:
   - Ad Formats: In-Feed Ads, Branded Hashtag Challenges, and TopView Ads (appear when users open the app).
   - Audience Engagement:
     - Focus on entertainment and authenticity to resonate with the platform's younger demographic.
     - Use trending audio, hashtags, and challenges to enhance visibility.
   - Creative Best Practices:
     - Short, vertical videos with eye-catching visuals and captions.
     - Emphasize storytelling and humor to connect with the audience.
3. LinkedIn:
   - Ad Formats: Sponsored Content, InMail Ads, and Lead Gen Forms.
   - Audience Targeting:
     - Target by industry, job title, seniority, and company size to reach professionals.
   - Key Use Cases:
     - B2B marketing, recruiting, and thought leadership campaigns.
   - Creative Best Practices:
     - Offer actionable insights, whitepapers, or case studies as lead magnets.
     - Use concise, professional copy and clean visuals.
4. Pinterest:

- Ad Formats: Promoted Pins, Idea Pins, and Shopping Ads.
- Audience Targeting: Focus on interests like home decor, fashion, and DIY.
- Creative Best Practices:
  - Use high-quality images and detailed descriptions.
  - Align with seasonal trends or events to increase engagement.

5. YouTube:
   - Ad Formats: Skippable and non-skippable ads, Bumper Ads, and Discovery Ads.
   - Audience Engagement:
     - Target by demographics, interests, and specific YouTube channels.
   - Creative Best Practices:
     - Keep the message clear in the first 5 seconds to capture attention.
     - Use compelling visuals and a strong CTA.

Dynamic and Shoppable Ads

Dynamic and shoppable ads enable brands to provide personalized and seamless shopping experiences directly within social media platforms.

1. Dynamic Ads:
   - Automatically adapt content to user behavior and preferences.
   - Examples:
     - Meta's Dynamic Ads: Show products users viewed on your website.
     - Google Discovery Ads: Deliver personalized product suggestions based on search history.
   - Best Practices:

- Use high-quality images and detailed product descriptions.
- Ensure product feeds are updated in real-time.

2. Shoppable Ads:
   - Allow users to purchase products directly from ads or social media posts.
   - Key Platforms:
     - Instagram: Shopping Tags, Shoppable Stories, and Live Shopping.
     - Pinterest: Buyable Pins with direct checkout options.
     - TikTok: Product links integrated into videos or profiles.
   - Best Practices:
   - Highlight price, availability, and key product features.
   - Use user-generated content (UGC) or influencer promotions to enhance credibility.

Measuring ROI in Social Media Ads

Measuring return on investment (ROI) is critical to understanding the effectiveness of your social media campaigns and optimizing future efforts.

1. Key Metrics:
   - Impressions and Reach: Measure the number of users who saw your ads.
   - Engagement Rate: Monitor likes, shares, comments, and click-through rates (CTR).
   - Conversion Rate: Track actions such as purchases, sign-ups, or downloads.
   - Cost Metrics:
     - CPC (Cost Per Click): Cost of each user

clicking on your ad.

- CPA (Cost Per Acquisition): Cost to acquire a customer or lead.
- ROAS (Return on Ad Spend): Calculate revenue generated versus advertising costs.

2. Attribution Models:

- Identify which channels or ads contribute to conversions using tools like Meta Attribution or Google Analytics.
- Use multi-touch attribution for a comprehensive understanding of the customer journey.

3. A/B Testing:

- Experiment with different ad creatives, copy, and CTAs to find the most effective combinations.
- Regularly analyze results to refine campaigns.

4. Analytics Tools:

- Use platform-native tools like Meta Ads Manager, TikTok Analytics, or LinkedIn Campaign Manager.
- Third-party solutions like Sprout Social or HubSpot for cross-platform analysis.

Social media advertising offers unmatched opportunities for engagement and conversion when strategies are tailored to platform strengths and audience preferences. Dynamic and shoppable ads further simplify the path to purchase, while precise ROI measurement ensures campaigns are optimized for success. Mastering these elements positions brands to thrive in the competitive digital landscape.

CHAPTER NINE
DATA-DRIVEN DECISION MAKING

Advanced Google Analytics

Google Analytics is an essential tool for tracking user behavior, measuring website performance, and making informed marketing decisions. Advanced features allow businesses to dig deeper into data for actionable insights.

1. Enhanced Tracking Capabilities:
   - Event Tracking: Monitor user interactions beyond page views, such as video plays, form submissions, and button clicks.
   - Cross-Domain Tracking: Track user behavior across multiple websites to gain a holistic view of the customer journey.
   - Custom Dimensions and Metrics: Tailor data collection to track specific user attributes or behaviors unique to your business.
2. Google Analytics 4 (GA4):
   - User-Centric Approach: GA4 focuses on user behavior across devices and platforms.
   - Predictive Metrics: Leverage AI-driven insights

such as purchase probability and revenue predictions.

- Event-Based Model: Move from session-based tracking to an event-based structure for greater granularity.

3. Segmentation and Audience Insights:
   - Use advanced segments to analyze specific user groups based on behavior, demographics, or acquisition source.
   - Combine insights with remarketing campaigns for targeted advertising.

4. Integration with Other Tools:
   - Connect Google Analytics with Google Ads, Search Console, and CRM platforms to consolidate data and measure campaign performance seamlessly.

Conversion Rate Optimization (CRO)

1. CRO focuses on increasing the percentage of website visitors who take desired actions, such as completing a purchase, filling out a form, or subscribing to a service.
2. CRO Framework:
3. Analyze: Use tools like heatmaps (Hotjar, Crazy Egg) and user session recordings to identify pain points.
4. Hypothesize: Develop data-backed hypotheses for improving the user experience.
5. Test: Implement A/B or multivariate testing to determine the effectiveness of changes.
6. Implement: Apply winning variations and monitor their performance over time.
7. Key Areas of Focus:

- Landing Pages:
  - Simplify navigation and use clear, compelling CTAs.
  - Optimize page load speed to reduce bounce rates.
- Forms:
  - Minimize required fields and ensure forms are mobile-friendly.
- Trust Signals:
  - Display customer reviews, certifications, and secure payment icons to build credibility.
8. Measuring CRO Success:
   - Track metrics like bounce rate, average session duration, and abandonment rates.
   - Use tools like Google Optimize or Optimizely for experimentation and analysis.

Predictive Analytics

Predictive analytics uses historical data, machine learning, and statistical algorithms to forecast future outcomes, helping businesses make proactive decisions.

1. Applications in Marketing:
   - Customer Behavior Predictions:
     - Forecast purchase likelihood or churn risk to guide retention strategies.
   - Personalization:
     - Tailor content and product recommendations based on predicted user preferences.
   - Ad Campaign Optimization:
     - Allocate budgets to high-performing campaigns or audiences identified through predictive modeling.
2. Tools for Predictive Analytics:

- Google Analytics Predictive Metrics: Predict purchase probability and revenue for specific user segments.
- CRM Tools: Platforms like Salesforce and HubSpot offer built-in predictive features for lead scoring and pipeline management.
- AI Platforms: Tools like IBM Watson and Tableau use machine learning to analyze and visualize predictive insights.

3. Predictive Modeling Techniques:
- Regression Analysis: Estimate relationships between variables to predict outcomes.
- Classification Models: Categorize users into groups, such as high-value customers or at-risk users.
- Time Series Analysis: Forecast trends based on temporal data.

4. Challenges and Best Practices:
- Ensure data quality by cleaning and normalizing datasets.
- Regularly validate predictive models to maintain accuracy.
- Balance automation with human oversight to interpret predictions effectively.

Data-driven decision-making empowers businesses to optimize their strategies through advanced analytics, CRO techniques, and predictive insights. By leveraging tools like Google Analytics, conducting rigorous testing, and applying machine learning models, marketers can anticipate user behavior and refine campaigns for maximum impact. In the competitive digital landscape, data is not just an advantage—it's a necessity for sustained success.

Part IV: Emerging Technologies and Trends

CHAPTER TEN
AI AND AUTOMATION IN DIGITAL MARKETING

Artificial Intelligence and Automation

Artificial intelligence (AI) and automation are revolutionizing digital marketing, enabling more personalized, efficient, and scalable strategies. Businesses leveraging these technologies can improve customer engagement, optimize campaigns, and stay ahead of competitors.

1. AI in Customer Insights:
   - AI-powered analytics tools like Google Analytics 4 and IBM Watson uncover patterns in consumer behavior, helping marketers predict trends and design targeted strategies.
   - Sentiment analysis tools (e.g., MonkeyLearn, Brandwatch) gauge customer opinions from social media and reviews.
2. AI in Campaign Optimization:
   - AI tools like Optmyzr and Adzooma dynamically adjust ad spend, targeting, and creatives for optimal ROI.
   - Predictive algorithms identify high-performing

audiences and anticipate campaign outcomes.
3. AI-Powered Content Creation:
   - Tools like Jasper and Writesonic generate high-quality, SEO-optimized content tailored to audience preferences.
   - Automated video creation platforms like Pictory streamline the production of engaging visual content.

Chatbots, AI Writers, and Personalization
1. Chatbots:
   - Role in Marketing:
   - Provide 24/7 customer support and answer FAQs.
   - Guide users through the sales funnel by offering product recommendations and solutions.
   - Examples:
   - Drift and Intercom enable conversational marketing through real-time customer interactions.
   - ChatGPT and similar tools power advanced, context-aware chatbots for deeper engagement.
   - Best Practices:
   - Integrate chatbots with CRM systems for seamless data exchange.
   - Personalize chatbot interactions based on user behavior and preferences.
2. AI Writers:
   - Capabilities:
   - Generate blog posts, product descriptions, and ad copy at scale.

- Improve efficiency while maintaining consistency in tone and style.
- Popular Tools:
  - Copy.ai, Jasper, and Writesonic for marketing copy and content creation.
- Challenges:
  - Balance AI-generated content with human editing to ensure authenticity and originality.
3. Personalization with AI:
  - AI-driven personalization tailors marketing messages to individual users based on behavior, preferences, and demographics.
  - Examples:
    - Netflix's recommendation engine suggests content based on viewing habits.
    - E-commerce platforms like Amazon deliver personalized product suggestions.
  - Implementation:
    - Use dynamic email campaigns with personalized subject lines and offers.
    - Implement product recommendation engines on websites and mobile apps.

Marketing Automation Platforms

Marketing automation platforms streamline repetitive tasks, improve efficiency, and enable sophisticated campaign management.
1. Key Features:
   - Lead Management: Automate lead scoring, nurturing, and segmentation.
   - Campaign Management: Schedule and manage multi-channel campaigns across email, social media, and ads.

- Analytics and Reporting: Gain insights into campaign performance with detailed dashboards and reports.
2. Top Marketing Automation Platforms:
   - HubSpot: Comprehensive tool for email marketing, CRM integration, and inbound campaigns.
   - Marketo: Advanced B2B-focused platform offering lead management and account-based marketing.
   - Pardot (Salesforce): Ideal for B2B companies seeking seamless Salesforce integration.
   - ActiveCampaign: Combines marketing automation with robust CRM features.
3. Benefits of Marketing Automation:
   - Scalability: Handle complex campaigns with minimal manual intervention.
   - Personalization: Deliver tailored content based on user interactions and preferences.
   - Efficiency: Automate repetitive tasks like email follow-ups, freeing up resources for strategic planning.
4. Best Practices:
   - Define clear goals and KPIs before implementing automation.
   - Maintain data hygiene to ensure accurate targeting and reporting.
   - Continuously analyze and refine automated workflows for maximum efficiency.

Emerging technologies like AI, chatbots, and marketing automation are reshaping the digital marketing landscape. By leveraging these innovations, businesses can enhance customer engagement, streamline operations, and achieve greater scalability. Staying informed about these trends and adopting the right tools will be critical for navigating the future of digital marketing successfully.

CHAPTER ELEVEN
THE METAVERSE AND DIGITAL MARKETING

Branding in Virtual Worlds

The metaverse, a digital realm combining augmented reality (AR), virtual reality (VR), and 3D virtual spaces, is emerging as a new frontier for digital marketing. As users increasingly engage in immersive, interactive environments, brands are finding innovative ways to connect with their audiences.

1. Establishing a Virtual Presence:
   - Companies can create branded spaces within the metaverse, such as virtual stores, event venues, or interactive experiences.
   - Examples:
     - Nike's "Nikeland" in Roblox: A virtual environment where users can explore branded content and activities.
     - Gucci Garden: An immersive virtual experience showcasing Gucci's brand story and products.
2. Interactive Brand Engagement:

- Enable users to engage with products or services through gamified experiences.
- Host events, concerts, or workshops to foster deeper emotional connections with audiences.
- Case Study: Balenciaga launched a virtual fashion show in a metaverse setting, allowing users to explore its latest collection.
3. Brand Consistency Across Channels:
   - Maintain cohesive branding between real-world and virtual experiences.
   - Integrate metaverse campaigns with social media, email, and traditional digital marketing to maximize impact.
4. Monetization Opportunities:
   - Sell virtual goods, like branded skins, accessories, or NFTs (non-fungible tokens), which users can purchase to enhance their digital identities.
   - Collaborate with creators and influencers native to the metaverse to amplify reach.

Advertising in AR/VR
1. Augmented Reality (AR) Advertising:
   - AR overlays digital elements onto the physical world, creating interactive and engaging ad experiences.
   - Applications:
     - Try-before-you-buy tools: Virtual fitting rooms or makeup try-on experiences.
     - Location-based campaigns: AR-powered scavenger hunts or promotional offers triggered by specific locations.
   - Examples:

- IKEA Place App: Allows users to visualize how furniture fits in their homes using AR.
- Snap Ads and AR Lenses: Interactive ad formats on Snapchat for engaging storytelling.

2. Virtual Reality (VR) Advertising:
- VR immerses users in a fully digital environment, offering unique opportunities for storytelling and experiential marketing.
- Applications:
  - Immersive storytelling: Create branded VR games or interactive stories.
  - Virtual product demonstrations: Allow users to explore and interact with products in 3D environments.
- Examples:
  - Audi VR Experience: A virtual test drive in a simulated environment.
  - Samsung Gear VR Ads: Immersive content showcasing the features of its latest products.

3. AR/VR Ad Formats:
- Branded Filters and Effects: Custom AR filters on platforms like Instagram, TikTok, and Snapchat.
- 360-Degree Video Ads: Interactive videos that allow users to explore a scene from all angles.
- In-VR Sponsorships: Placement of branded elements in virtual worlds or games.

Challenges and Opportunities
1. Challenges:
- Cost: Developing AR/VR content can be resource-intensive.
- Adoption Barriers: Not all users have access to

AR/VR devices, limiting reach.
- Measurement: Tracking the ROI of metaverse campaigns requires new metrics and tools.
2. Opportunities:
   - Early Adoption Advantage: Brands entering the metaverse now can establish themselves as innovators.
   - High Engagement: Immersive experiences foster deeper connections compared to traditional ads.
   - Data Insights: User interactions within virtual environments provide valuable data for personalization and campaign refinement.

The metaverse and AR/VR technologies are opening up exciting possibilities for brands to engage with consumers in immersive, innovative ways. By embracing these platforms, companies can create memorable experiences, enhance brand loyalty, and position themselves as pioneers in the next wave of digital marketing. While challenges exist, the potential for impactful storytelling and interaction makes exploring this space essential for forward-thinking marketers.

CHAPTER TWELVE
BLOCKCHAIN AND DIGITAL MARKETING

Smart Contracts in Advertising

Blockchain technology, originally developed for cryptocurrency, is transforming digital marketing by enhancing transparency, security, and trust. Its decentralized nature ensures that data is immutable and accessible, making it a game-changer for advertising, campaign management, and consumer trust.

What Are Smart Contracts?

Smart contracts are self-executing agreements with terms written in code, running on blockchain networks like Ethereum. They automatically enforce obligations, reducing the need for intermediaries in transactions.

1. Applications in Digital Advertising:
   - Payment Automation:
     - Advertisers and publishers can use smart contracts to automate payments based on predefined metrics, such as clicks, impressions, or conversions.
     - Eliminates delays and disputes over ad

payments.
- Fraud Prevention:
  - Smart contracts verify ad delivery before payments are made, reducing instances of click fraud and fake impressions.
- Programmatic Advertising:
  - Smart contracts streamline real-time bidding (RTB) by executing transactions directly between advertisers and ad platforms, bypassing middlemen.
2. Examples of Smart Contracts in Action:
  - Amino Payments: Uses blockchain to ensure transparency in programmatic ad spending.
  - Basic Attention Token (BAT): A blockchain-based digital advertising platform where users earn tokens for viewing ads, and advertisers pay only for verified user attention.

Transparency and Trust in Digital Campaigns
1. Eliminating Ad Fraud:
  - Blockchain can verify the authenticity of ad impressions, ensuring that advertisers only pay for real user engagement.
  - Examples include verifying user identity without compromising privacy and validating publisher traffic sources.
2. Improved Data Privacy:
  - Blockchain gives users greater control over their personal data, allowing them to share it selectively with advertisers.
  - Decentralized Identity (DID) systems ensure user anonymity while maintaining data integrity.
3. Supply Chain Transparency:

- Blockchain provides an immutable record of transactions, allowing advertisers to trace every dollar spent.
- Reduces wastage and ensures funds are allocated efficiently to campaigns.
- Example: MetaX's "adChain" creates a transparent digital ad supply chain.

4. Enhanced Brand Trust:
   - Transparent blockchain records foster trust between brands and consumers.
   - Consumers can verify the authenticity of campaigns, such as charitable donations tied to purchase actions.

5. Loyalty Programs and Tokenization:
   - Blockchain enables brands to create tokenized loyalty programs, where customers earn blockchain-based tokens for purchases or engagements.
   - These tokens can be redeemed across multiple platforms, fostering cross-brand collaborations.
   - Example: Starbucks' blockchain-based loyalty program for rewarding regular customers.

Challenges and Considerations

1. Technical Complexity:
   - Implementing blockchain solutions requires specialized expertise, which may be a barrier for smaller businesses.

2. Scalability Issues:
   - Blockchain networks can face scalability challenges, particularly with high transaction volumes.

3. Regulatory Concerns:

- The legal landscape surrounding blockchain and data privacy is still evolving, creating potential compliance risks.
4. Cost:
   - Initial implementation of blockchain-based solutions can be expensive, though long-term benefits may outweigh costs.

Future Opportunities
1. Blockchain-Driven Marketplaces:
   - Decentralized ad exchanges where advertisers and publishers transact directly, eliminating intermediaries.
2. Proof-of-Origin Campaigns:
   - Use blockchain to verify the ethical sourcing of products or sustainability claims, appealing to socially conscious consumers.
3. Real-Time Campaign Monitoring:
   - Blockchain's transparency allows marketers to monitor campaign performance in real time, ensuring accurate ROI calculations.

Blockchain technology offers significant advantages for digital marketing by fostering transparency, trust, and efficiency. From automating ad payments with smart contracts to creating transparent ad supply chains, blockchain has the potential to address many longstanding challenges in the industry. As adoption increases, businesses that embrace blockchain innovations will position themselves as leaders in the future of digital marketing.

Part V: Strategy and Implementation

CHAPTER THIRTEEN
BUILDING A DIGITAL MARKETING STRATEGY

A well-rounded digital marketing strategy aligns business goals with actionable tactics to reach target audiences effectively. It requires a thorough understanding of market dynamics, customer personas, and available channels.

1. Defining Your Vision and Objectives:
   - Start with a clear understanding of your business's mission and how digital marketing supports it.
   - Examples of objectives include increasing brand awareness, generating leads, driving sales, or enhancing customer retention.
2. Understanding Your Audience:
   - Develop detailed buyer personas by analyzing demographic, psychographic, and behavioral data.
   - Use tools like Google Analytics, CRM systems, and social media insights for data-driven personas.

3. Choosing the Right Channels:
   - Identify the most effective platforms for your audience (e.g., Instagram for younger demographics, LinkedIn for B2B professionals).
   - Balance organic and paid efforts across content, social, email, and paid media.
4. Competitor Analysis:
   - Benchmark against competitors to understand strengths, weaknesses, and opportunities.
   - Tools like SEMrush and SimilarWeb can help analyze competitors' digital presence.
5. Integrating All Components:
   - Combine SEO, content marketing, social media, email, and paid campaigns into a cohesive strategy.
   - Ensure messaging is consistent across all channels for a seamless customer experience.

Goal Setting and KPIs
1. Setting SMART Goals:
   - Specific: Clearly define what you aim to achieve (e.g., "Increase website traffic by 25% in 6 months").
   - Measurable: Use data and metrics to track progress.
   - Achievable: Ensure goals are realistic given available resources.
   - Relevant: Align goals with broader business objectives.
   - Time-Bound: Set a deadline for achieving each goal.
2. Identifying Key Performance Indicators (KPIs):
   - Awareness Stage: Metrics like impressions,

reach, and website visits.
- Consideration Stage: Engagement rates, click-through rates (CTR), and time on site.
- Decision Stage: Conversion rates, cost per acquisition (CPA), and ROI.
- Retention Stage: Customer lifetime value (CLV) and churn rate.
3. Tracking Progress:
- Use analytics platforms (e.g., Google Analytics, HubSpot) to monitor KPIs in real time.
- Regularly review and adjust goals based on campaign performance and market trends.

Budgeting and Resource Allocation
1. Determining Your Budget:
- Allocate a percentage of your revenue to digital marketing based on industry standards (e.g., 5–15% for most industries).
- Balance long-term investments (SEO, content) with short-term tactics (PPC, social ads).
2. Breaking Down Costs:
- Content Creation: Blog writing, video production, graphic design.
- Ad Spend: Budgets for platforms like Google Ads, Facebook, and TikTok.
- Tools and Software: Subscriptions to tools like SEMrush, Hootsuite, or marketing automation platforms.
- Training and Development: Resources for team skill enhancement and certification programs.

3. Allocating Resources Effectively:
- Divide efforts across in-house teams,

freelancers, or agencies based on expertise and workload.
- Use a project management tool like Asana or Trello to streamline workflows.
4. Evaluating ROI:
   - Track ROI for each channel and adjust allocations based on performance.
   - Example: Increase PPC spend if it generates a higher return compared to email campaigns.

Building a successful digital marketing strategy involves careful planning, measurable goal-setting, and efficient allocation of resources. By focusing on your target audience, selecting the right channels, and continually analyzing performance, you can create impactful campaigns that drive real business results. Effective budgeting and clear KPIs ensure your efforts remain sustainable and scalable over time.

CHAPTER FOURTEEN
INTEGRATED MARKETING COMMUNICATIONS (IMC)

Integrated Marketing Communications (IMC) is the practice of harmonizing all marketing channels and tools to deliver a unified, consistent message. It ensures that audiences experience seamless interactions with a brand, whether online or offline, enhancing brand recognition and driving loyalty.

Creating Omnichannel Experiences
1. What Are Omnichannel Experiences?
   - Omnichannel marketing ensures customers receive a cohesive experience across all touchpoints, including websites, social media, email, in-store, and customer service interactions.
   - Focus is on maintaining consistent messaging, design, and user experience (UX) across the customer journey.
2. Steps to Create Omnichannel Experiences:
   - Understand Your Customer Journey:
   - Map out how customers interact with your brand across channels.

- Unify Customer Data:
- Leverage CRM platforms to collect and analyze data from various touchpoints for a single customer view.
- Personalize Interactions:
- Use data insights to deliver tailored messages based on user preferences and behavior.
- Optimize for Mobile:
- Ensure mobile-responsive designs and mobile-first strategies as most users engage through their smartphones.
- Seamless Transitions:
- Integrate touchpoints to allow users to switch channels without losing context. For example, an online cart should sync with an in-store app.
3. Examples of Omnichannel Strategies:
   - Starbucks Rewards: A customer can check their balance or redeem rewards through the app, website, or in-store, ensuring a seamless loyalty experience.
   - Nike App Integration: Combines online shopping, in-store visits, and personalized workout content into one cohesive ecosystem.

Aligning Online and Offline Campaigns
1. Why Integration Matters:
   - While digital campaigns reach a vast audience, offline campaigns like events or print ads provide tangible interactions. Aligning both maximizes impact and reinforces brand messaging.
2. Strategies for Integration:
   - Consistent Branding:

- Ensure logos, color schemes, and messaging are uniform across all mediums.
- Drive Traffic Between Channels:
  - Use QR codes in offline ads to direct users to your website or app.
  - Promote in-store offers through email or social media.
- Leverage Local Campaigns:
  - Tailor campaigns to regional preferences while maintaining global brand alignment.
  - Example: Coca-Cola's personalized bottle campaigns combined print ads with online social sharing.
- Event-Based Marketing:
  - Synchronize live events (trade shows, product launches) with digital coverage through social media and live streaming.

Case Studies
- Apple: Combines online ads, email marketing, and physical stores to deliver a cohesive product launch experience. Online pre-orders, in-store pickups, and consistent branding amplify the impact.
- IKEA: Links its printed catalog to its AR app, allowing users to visualize furniture in their homes, merging offline discovery with digital interactivity.

Challenges and Solutions
1. Challenge: Fragmented Customer Data
   - Solution: Adopt centralized CRM and analytics platforms to unify data.

2. Challenge: Inconsistent Messaging Across Teams
   - Solution: Develop comprehensive brand guidelines and provide training for all marketing teams.
3. Challenge: Technological Barriers
   - Solution: Invest in technology that integrates marketing channels, such as marketing automation platforms.

Integrated Marketing Communications ensures that all customer interactions with a brand are cohesive, regardless of the channel. By focusing on omnichannel strategies and aligning online and offline campaigns, businesses can enhance customer engagement and reinforce their brand identity. In today's fragmented media landscape, IMC is not just a strategy but a necessity for staying relevant and competitive.

CHAPTER FIFTEEN
GLOBAL MARKETING AND LOCALIZATION

In an increasingly interconnected world, businesses often aim to reach diverse audiences across the globe. However, success in international markets requires more than translating campaigns; it demands an understanding of local cultures, behaviors, and preferences. This chapter delves into tailoring global campaigns for local audiences and overcoming cultural and linguistic barriers.

Tailoring Campaigns to Local Markets
1. Understanding Market Nuances:
   - Conduct market research to identify local consumer preferences, buying behaviors, and economic conditions.
   - Leverage data from surveys, focus groups, and regional analytics tools to uncover insights.
2. Adapting Marketing Strategies:
   - Localized Content:
     - Create content that reflects the local culture, language, and societal values.
     - Use examples, idioms, and visuals that

resonate with regional audiences.
- Pricing Strategies:
  - Adjust pricing models to align with local economic conditions and purchasing power.
- Product Customization:
  - Modify products to suit regional needs. For instance, McDonald's offers vegetarian options in India to cater to dietary norms.
3. Choosing the Right Channels:
  - Identify the most popular digital and traditional platforms in the region.
  - Example: Use WeChat and Baidu in China, while leveraging WhatsApp and Instagram in Latin America.
4. Case Study:
  - Coca-Cola's "Share a Coke" Campaign:
  - Names on bottles were customized to reflect popular names in each region, making the campaign globally adaptable yet locally relevant.

Overcoming Cultural and Linguistic Barriers
1. Understanding Cultural Sensitivities:
  - Research cultural norms, taboos, and societal values to avoid offensive or inappropriate messaging.
  - Consider the role of religion, family structures, and social hierarchies in decision-making.
  - Example: Colors have different connotations— white symbolizes purity in Western cultures but mourning in parts of Asia.
2. Language Localization:
  - Translation vs. Transcreation:

- Translation converts text literally, while transcreation adapts messages to preserve context, tone, and intent.
- Example: KFC's "Finger-Lickin' Good" was transcreated in Chinese to avoid its initial mistranslation as "Eat Your Fingers Off."
- Collaborate with native speakers and linguists to ensure accuracy and cultural alignment.

3. Leveraging Local Influencers:
- Partner with regional influencers who understand the local audience and can amplify your message authentically.
- Example: Use micro-influencers on TikTok for younger demographics in Japan versus professional LinkedIn influencers for a B2B campaign in Germany.

4. Navigating Regulatory Environments:
- Understand local laws governing advertising, data privacy, and consumer protection.
- Example: Complying with GDPR in Europe or ad restrictions for alcohol and tobacco in certain countries.

Strategies for Effective Localization

1. Hire Local Experts:
- Collaborate with local marketing teams or agencies who understand the market dynamics and cultural subtleties.

2. Test Campaigns Before Full Launch:
- Conduct A/B testing to gauge how messages resonate with local audiences.
- Use focus groups or pilot programs to refine campaigns.

3. Maintain Brand Consistency:
   - Ensure that localized campaigns align with the core brand identity while catering to local preferences.
   - Example: Nike's "Just Do It" slogan remains consistent globally, but ads reflect diverse athletic aspirations in each region.
4. Leverage Technology:
   - Use AI-powered tools for real-time translation, audience segmentation, and cultural trend analysis.
   - Tools like Smartling or Phrase can streamline content localization processes.

Challenges and Solutions
1. Challenge: Balancing Global Consistency with Local Relevance
   - Solution: Develop a flexible global framework with room for local adaptations.
2. Challenge: Limited Knowledge of Local Markets
   - Solution: Invest in research and hire consultants or agencies with regional expertise.
3. Challenge: Budget Constraints for Localization
   - Solution: Prioritize high-impact regions and scale campaigns based on ROI.

Global marketing success hinges on the ability to tailor campaigns to the unique characteristics of local markets while maintaining the integrity of the global brand. By addressing cultural and linguistic barriers, businesses can foster deeper connections with regional audiences, driving growth and brand loyalty in diverse markets.

Part VI:
Specialized Areas and Ethical Considerations

CHAPTER SIXTEEN
B2B VS. B2C DIGITAL MARKETING

B2B (Business-to-Business) and B2C (Business-to-Consumer) marketing operate within distinct paradigms, each requiring tailored strategies, content styles, and engagement methods.

Key Differences Between B2B and B2C Marketing
1. Target Audiences:
   - B2B: The audience comprises businesses, industry professionals, and decision-makers. These individuals prioritize ROI, efficiency, and professional credibility in their purchasing decisions.
   - B2C: Consumers are the primary audience, driven by personal needs, desires, and emotions. The buying process is often quicker and less formal.
2. Decision-Making Processes:
   - B2B: Purchases are collaborative, often involving multiple stakeholders, detailed research, and a longer sales cycle.
   - B2C: The process is usually individual-driven,

emotional, and influenced by marketing triggers such as promotions and recommendations.

3. Content Style:
   - B2B: Focuses on educational and informative content like whitepapers, case studies, and webinars.
   - B2C: Relies on visually engaging, entertaining, and emotionally appealing content.

Best Practices for B2B Marketing
- Leverage LinkedIn and Industry Platforms: LinkedIn is invaluable for B2B marketers, offering tools to connect with professionals and share thought leadership.
- Focus on Account-Based Marketing (ABM): Tailor content and outreach to key accounts to maximize relevance.
- Showcase Expertise: Demonstrate value through comprehensive guides, data-backed reports, and success stories.

Best Practices for B2C Marketing
- Engage with Visual Storytelling: Platforms like Instagram, TikTok, and Facebook thrive on visually appealing content.
- Incentivize Purchases: Discounts, limited-time offers, and loyalty programs drive conversions.
- Harness User-Generated Content: Encourage customers to share their experiences for authentic brand advocacy.

Case Study Comparisons

- B2B: Salesforce's use of in-depth webinars and customer success stories to appeal to decision-makers in large enterprises.
- B2C: Nike's powerful, emotion-driven campaigns like "Just Do It," resonating with individual aspirations globally.

CHAPTER SEVENTEEN
ETHICAL DIGITAL MARKETING

Ethical digital marketing is foundational for building trust and long-term relationships with consumers. In a world of heightened scrutiny, businesses must balance their marketing objectives with responsible practices.

Data Privacy and GDPR Compliance
1. The Importance of Data Privacy:
    - Consumers expect transparency about how their data is collected, used, and stored. Breaches in trust can lead to reputational damage and legal consequences.
2. Understanding GDPR:
    - The General Data Protection Regulation (GDPR) mandates that businesses operating in the EU or handling EU citizens' data must ensure:
        - Explicit consent for data collection.
        - Secure storage and processing of personal data.
        - Clear opt-out mechanisms.
3. Compliance Best Practices:

- Use plain language to explain data policies.
- Regularly audit your data handling processes.
- Appoint a Data Protection Officer (DPO) for accountability.

Responsible Advertising

1. Avoid Manipulative Practices:
   - Do not exploit user vulnerabilities with dark patterns, misleading claims, or intrusive ads.
2. Foster Transparency:
   - Clearly label sponsored content and disclose partnerships.
3. Examples of Responsibility in Action:
   - Patagonia's commitment to sustainable advertising that aligns with their environmental mission.

CHAPTER EIGHTEEN
CRISIS MANAGEMENT IN THE DIGITAL AGE

The rapid dissemination of information in the digital world means that crises can escalate quickly. Effective crisis management ensures brands can mitigate damage and maintain trust.

Handling Social Media Backlash
1. Acknowledging the Problem:
   - Respond promptly and empathetically to public concerns. Ignoring or dismissing issues often exacerbates them.
2. Transparency in Communication:
   - Share accurate information about the issue, steps being taken to resolve it, and timelines for action.
3. Examples of Successful Crisis Responses:
   - Starbucks demonstrated swift action and commitment to inclusivity after facing allegations of racial discrimination in their stores.

Proactive Reputation Management
1. Monitoring Online Sentiment:

- Use tools like Google Alerts, Brandwatch, or Hootsuite to track mentions and sentiment around your brand.
2. Building a Positive Digital Footprint:
   - Invest in corporate social responsibility (CSR) initiatives and promote them through social media.
3. Prevention Through Preparation:
   - Develop a crisis response plan outlining potential risks, designated spokespersons, and escalation procedures.

Post-Crisis Actions
1. Evaluate the Response:
   - Assess what worked and what didn't in managing the crisis.
2. Rebuild Trust:
   - Engage in community outreach or customer appreciation campaigns to reinforce a positive brand image.

The specialized nature of B2B and B2C marketing requires distinct approaches, but both benefit from a foundation of ethical practices and thoughtful strategies. By adhering to data privacy laws, promoting responsible advertising, and maintaining robust crisis management plans, businesses can navigate challenges effectively while fostering trust and loyalty in a dynamic digital environment.

CHAPTER NINETEEN
CASE STUDIES AND LESSONS

Digital marketing is both an art and a science, and some of the best lessons come from analyzing real-world examples. This section delves into case studies from leading brands, identifying what made their campaigns successful and the mistakes others can learn to avoid. It also explores the future of digital marketing, highlighting emerging trends and how businesses can prepare for upcoming disruptions.

Case Studies from Leading Brands
1. Nike: The "Dream Crazy" Campaign
   Overview:
   In 2018, Nike launched the "Dream Crazy" campaign featuring Colin Kaepernick, leveraging the athlete's polarizing activism to spark conversation. The campaign encouraged audiences to "believe in something, even if it means sacrificing everything."
   - Key Strategies:
     - Emotionally charged storytelling that resonated with Nike's core values of

empowerment and courage.

- A bold stance on a social issue that generated widespread discussion, even controversy.
- Integration across platforms, including TV, social media, and print, ensuring maximum reach.
- Results:
- A 31% increase in online sales within days of the campaign's launch.
- Unprecedented engagement and earned media coverage.
- Takeaway:
- Authentic alignment between a brand's values and its messaging can drive loyalty, even at the risk of alienating some audiences.

2. Coca-Cola: "Share a Coke" Campaign
Overview:
Coca-Cola personalized its products by replacing its iconic logo with popular first names in various countries.

- Key Strategies:
- Personalization at scale: Printing common names ensured a broad appeal while encouraging individual connections.
- Encouragement of user-generated content, with consumers sharing photos of their personalized bottles on social media.
- Localization: Names were tailored to cultural and regional preferences.
- Results:
- Sales increased by over 2% in key markets,

reversing declining consumption trends.
- The campaign became a global phenomenon, implemented in over 80 countries.
- Takeaway:
- Personalized marketing can forge deeper emotional connections, turning products into experiences.

3. Old Spice: "The Man Your Man Could Smell Like"
Overview:
Old Spice rebranded its image with a humorous and engaging campaign targeting women as influencers of male grooming purchases.
- Key Strategies:
- Witty and surreal humor that captivated audiences.
- Interactive elements, including real-time responses to fan comments through personalized video replies.
- A strong focus on social media platforms like YouTube and Twitter.
- Results:
- A 125% increase in sales in the first six months of the campaign.
- Over 105 million video views, establishing Old Spice as a digital marketing powerhouse.
- Takeaway:
- Engaging content paired with interactivity can reinvigorate a legacy brand.

Lessons from Successful Campaigns
Analyzing successful campaigns reveals common principles that marketers can replicate:
1. Customer-Centric Strategies:

- Put the audience's needs, values, and preferences at the center of the campaign.
- Example: Amazon's use of AI for personalized product recommendations.

2. Leveraging Emotional Appeal:
- Campaigns that evoke strong emotions—whether joy, nostalgia, or inspiration—leave lasting impressions.
- Example: Google's "Parisian Love" ad, which told a love story through search queries.

3. Adaptability and Innovation:
- Brands that innovate and embrace new trends stay relevant.
- Example: Wendy's humorous and snarky Twitter strategy, which boosted brand engagement.

Common Pitfalls and How to Avoid Them

Even the most seasoned marketers make mistakes. Avoiding these pitfalls can save brands from costly missteps.

1. Lack of Authenticity:
- Example: Pepsi's tone-deaf ad featuring Kendall Jenner trivialized social justice issues, sparking widespread criticism.
- Solution: Ensure campaigns align with your brand's identity and respect cultural sensitivities.

2. Neglecting Data Privacy:
- Example: Cambridge Analytica's misuse of Facebook user data led to public outcry and regulatory scrutiny.
- Solution: Prioritize transparency and compliance with privacy laws like GDPR and

CCPA.

3. Failing to Measure ROI:
   - Many campaigns falter because they lack clear goals or metrics.
   - Solution: Set specific KPIs, such as engagement rates, lead conversions, or customer retention, and track them rigorously.

CHAPTER TWENTY
THE FUTURE OF DIGITAL MARKETING

The digital marketing landscape is evolving rapidly. To remain competitive, businesses must anticipate and adapt to new technologies and consumer behaviors.

Emerging Trends and Technologies
1. Artificial Intelligence (AI):
   - AI will continue to transform marketing, from predictive analytics to hyper-personalized customer experiences.
   - Example: ChatGPT for content creation and conversational marketing.
2. Augmented Reality (AR) and Virtual Reality (VR):
   - Brands will leverage AR/VR for immersive shopping experiences.
   - Example: IKEA's AR app, which lets users visualize furniture in their homes.
3. Voice Search and Smart Assistants:
   - Optimizing for voice search will become critical as devices like Alexa and Google Home gain adoption.

Preparing for the Next Wave of Disruption
1. Invest in Continuous Learning:
   - Stay updated on industry trends through courses, conferences, and certifications.
2. Experiment with New Platforms:
   - Early adopters of platforms like Threads or emerging technologies gain a competitive edge.
3. Prioritize Sustainability:
   - Consumers increasingly prefer brands with sustainable practices. Ensure your marketing aligns with environmental values.

By examining real-world successes and failures, marketers gain a clearer understanding of what works in the dynamic digital landscape. As new technologies emerge and consumer expectations shift, the future of digital marketing will be shaped by those who innovate while staying rooted in ethical and customer-centric practices.

APPENDICES

APPENDIX A
TOOLS AND PLATFORMS FOR DIGITAL MARKETERS

Having the right tools is essential to streamline workflows, improve campaign performance, and achieve measurable results. This section highlights a comprehensive list of digital marketing tools, categorized by their use cases.

Content Creation and Management
- Canva: Ideal for creating social media graphics, infographics, and presentations. Offers templates for quick designs.
- Adobe Creative Cloud (Photoshop, Premiere Pro, etc.): Industry-standard tools for advanced graphic design, video editing, and animation.
- WordPress: A versatile content management system (CMS) for building and managing blogs and websites.
- Lumen5: Transforms written content into engaging videos using AI.
- Grammarly: Proofreading and eciting tool to refine written content.

SEO and Analytics

- Google Analytics 4: Provides in-depth website performance insights, including traffic sources and user behavior.
- SEMrush: An all-in-one SEO platform for keyword research, competitor analysis, and content optimization.
- Ahrefs: A robust tool for backlink tracking, rank monitoring, and content gap analysis.
- Screaming Frog: A website crawler that helps identify technical SEO issues.
- Yoast SEO: WordPress plugin for on-page SEO optimization.

Social Media Management Tools

- Hootsuite: Schedule posts, track engagement, and monitor social conversations across platforms.
- Sprout Social: Offers analytics, social listening, and content scheduling in one platform.
- Later: Focused on visual-first platforms like Instagram and Pinterest, with drag-and-drop scheduling features.
- Brandwatch: For social listening and sentiment analysis

Email Marketing

- Mailchimp: Ideal for small to medium-sized businesses, offering automation and segmentation tools.
- HubSpot: A robust platform integrating email with CRM, analytics, and inbound marketing.
- Constant Contact: User-friendly platform for newsletters and email campaigns.

Advertising and PPC

- Google Ads: The cornerstone of paid search advertising.
- Meta Ads Manager: Create and manage campaigns across Facebook and Instagram.
- AdRoll: Focused on retargeting and dynamic display ads.
- LinkedIn Ads: A platform for B2B lead generation and professional audience targeting.

Collaboration and Productivity
- Asana: Manage marketing projects and tasks efficiently.
- Trello: Visual task management through boards and cards.
- Slack: Streamline team communication.
- Smartsheet: Comprehensive tool for marketing project management and reporting.

APPENDIX B
GLOSSARY OF DIGITAL MARKETING TERMS

The world of digital marketing is rife with jargon. This glossary provides clear definitions to demystify key terms.

Essential Terms

1. A/B Testing: Comparing two versions of a web page, email, or ad to determine which performs better.
2. Algorithm: A set of rules social media platforms or search engines use to rank content.
3. Attribution Model: A framework for assigning credit to various touchpoints in a customer's journey.
4. Bounce Rate: The percentage of visitors who leave a website after viewing only one page.
5. Call-to-Action (CTA): A prompt that encourages users to take a specific action, such as "Buy Now" or "Learn More."
6. Conversion Rate: The percentage of users who complete a desired action, like making a purchase or filling out a form.
7. Engagement Rate: Measures interactions (likes,

comments, shares) relative to the audience size.

8. Impression: The number of times an ad or piece of content is displayed to users.
9. Organic Reach: The number of people who see your content without paid promotion.
10. PPC (Pay-Per-Click): An advertising model where advertisers pay each time a user clicks their ad.
11. Retargeting: Serving ads to users who have previously interacted with your brand.
12. SEO (Search Engine Optimization): Strategies to improve a website's visibility in organic search results.

APPENDIX C
TEMPLATES AND FRAMEWORKS

This section provides practical templates and frameworks that you can directly implement in your campaigns.

Content Calendar Template

Objective: Organize and schedule your content creation and publishing process.

Date	Plat-form	Content Type	Post Cap-tion/ Title	Visual/ Asset	Status	Metrics to Track
Jan 10, 2025	Insta-gram	Carou-sel Post	"Top Mar-keting Tips"	Canva Design #3	Sched-uled	Engage-ment, Reach
Jan 12, 2025	Blog	Article	"SEO Trends 2025"	Blog Hero Image	Drafted	Traffic, Shares

SEO Audit Checklist

Goal: Ensure your website is optimized for search

engines.

1. Technical SEO:
   - Check site speed using Google PageSpeed Insights.
   - Ensure mobile responsiveness.
   - Audit site architecture for crawlability and proper indexing.
2. On-Page SEO:
   - Optimize title tags, meta descriptions, and headers.
   - Use target keywords naturally within content.
   - Ensure image alt texts are descriptive.
3. Content Strategy:
   - Update old blog posts with new data and keywords.
   - Use internal links to guide users and boost SEO.
4. Backlink Profile:
   - Use tools like Ahrefs to identify toxic backlinks.
   - Focus on acquiring high-quality backlinks.

Digital Marketing Budget Template

Purpose: Allocate resources effectively across campaigns.

Category	Budget Allocated	Budget Spent	ROI
Google Ads	$5,000	$4,800	3x
Social Media Advertising	$3,000	$2,700	2.5x
Content Creation	$2,000	$1,800	N/A

Crisis Management Playbook

Objective: Respond swiftly and effectively to online crises.

1. Identify the Crisis:
   - Monitor social media mentions and customer complaints using tools like Brandwatch.
2. Assemble a Crisis Team:
   - Designate roles (spokesperson, social media manager, legal advisor).
3. Craft a Transparent Response:
   - Acknowledge the issue, outline corrective steps, and communicate timelines.
4. Monitor Sentiment:
   - Use sentiment analysis tools to gauge public reaction.
5. Post-Crisis Review:
   - Analyze the root cause, document lessons learned, and update processes to prevent recurrence.

These appendices are practical, hands-on resources for marketers aiming to improve efficiency and effectiveness. From tools to manage campaigns, a glossary for clear communication, and actionable templates, this section ensures you have everything you need to excel in digital marketing.